OLD TIME ROCK 'N' ROLL

ISBN 0-7935-4433-5

HAL•LEONARD® CORPORATION

7777 W. BLUEMOUND RD. P.O. BOX 13819 MILWAUKEE, WI 53213

OLD TIME ROCK 'N' ROLL

CONTENTS

BAND OF GOLD

Words and Music by EDYTHE WAYNE
and RONALD DUNBAR

5

tried be - fore. _ Since you've been gone _____ all that's left __ is a

band of gold, all that's left __ of the dreams I hold __ is a

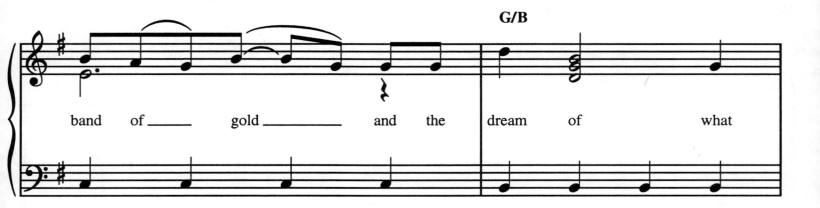

band of _____ gold _____ and the dream of what

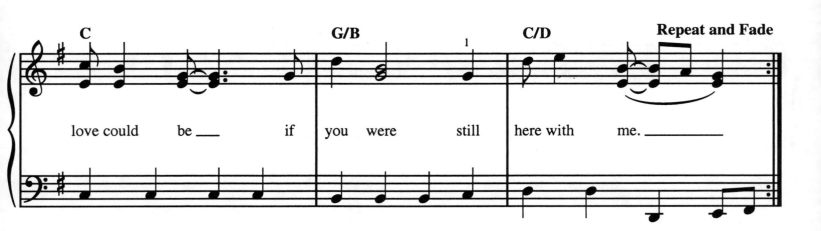

love could be __ if you were still here with me. _____

BITS AND PIECES

Words and Music by
DAVE CLARK and MIKE SMITH

THE BIRDS AND THE BEES

Words and Music by
HERB NEWMAN

BLUE SUEDE SHOES

Words and Music by
CARL LEE PERKINS

17

uh   uh,   hon-ey, lay   off of my shoes. _   Don't   you

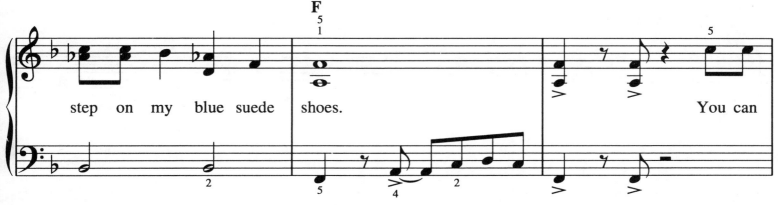

step   on   my   blue suede   shoes.   You can

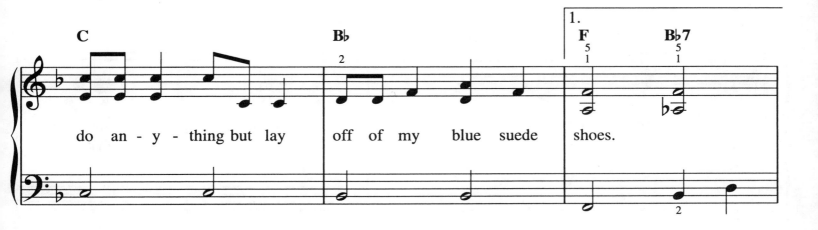

do   an-y-thing but lay   off of my   blue suede   shoes.

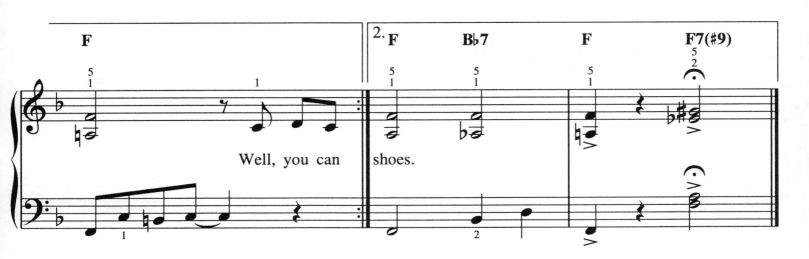

Well, you can   shoes.

BOBBY'S GIRL

Words and Music by GARY KLEIN
and HENRY HOFFMAN

Moderately

With light pedal

When peo - ple
Each night I

ask of me ____
sit at home ____

what would you
hop - ing that

like to be, ____
he will phone, ____

now that you're
but I know

BREAKING UP IS HARD TO DO

Words and Music by HOWARD GREENFIELD
and NEIL SEDAKA

25

CALENDAR GIRL

Words and Music by HOWARD GREENFIELD
and NEIL SEDAKA

28

C

(March) I'm gon - na march you down the aisle, ___
ly) Like a fire cracker I'm a - glow, ___

Am

(A - pril) You're the Eas - ter bun - ny when you smile. ___
(Aug - ust) When you're on the beach you steal the show. _

F   **F#dim**   **C/G**

Yeah,   yeah,   my heart's in a whirl. ___   I   love, I love, I love my lit - tle

A7   **D7**   **G7**

cal - en - dar girl ___ ev - 'ry day, _____ ev - 'ry day ___ of the ___

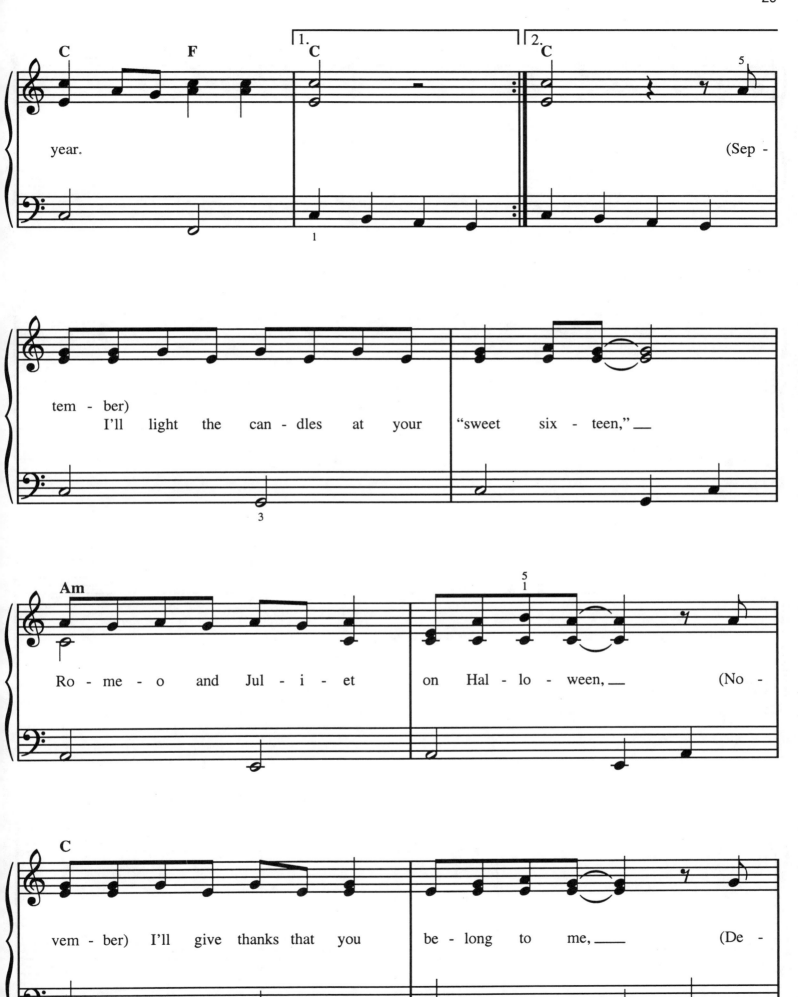

CARA, MIA

By JULIO TRAPANI
and LEE LANGE

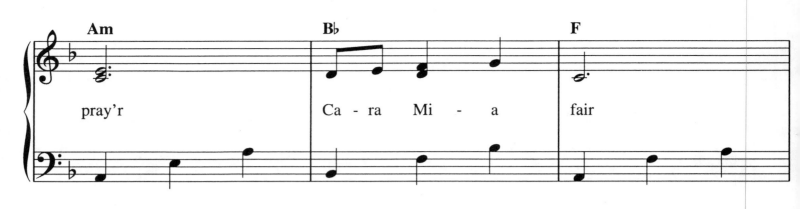

pray'r   Ca - ra   Mi - a   fair

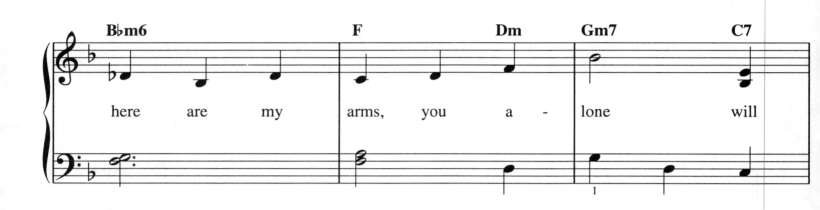

here   are   my   arms,   you   a -   lone   will

share.   All   I   want   is   you   for

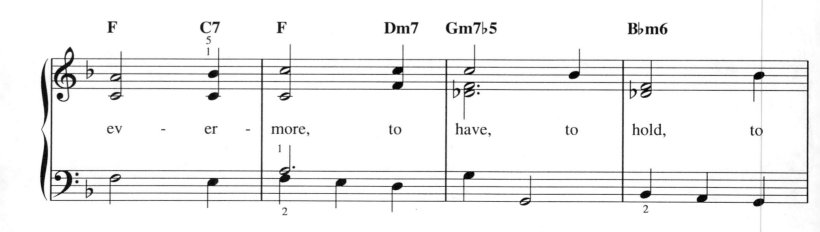

ev - er - more,   to   have,   to   hold,   to

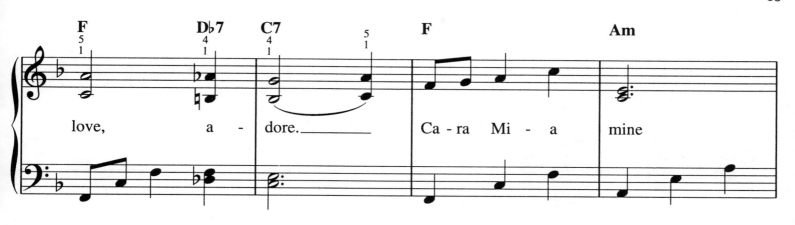

love,   a -   dore._____   Ca - ra   Mi - a   mine

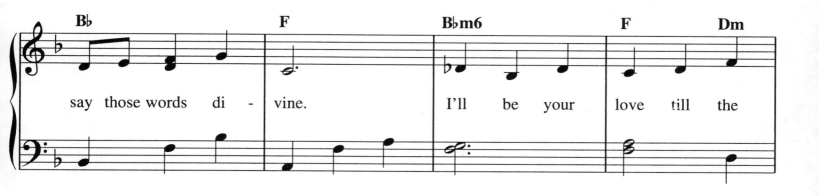

say those words di - vine.   I'll   be   your   love   till   the

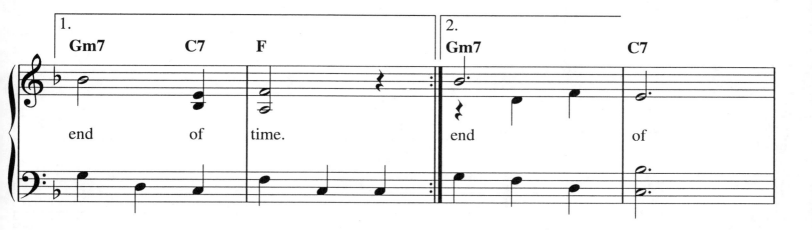

end   of   time.   end   of

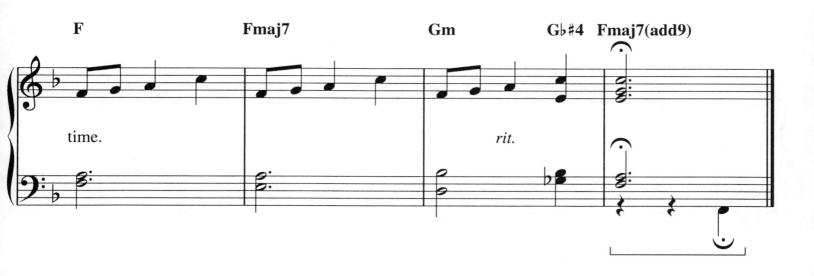

time.   *rit.*

CAN'T BUY ME LOVE

Words and Music by JOHN LENNON
and PAUL McCARTNEY

35

thing, my friend, if it makes you feel al - right.}
lot to give, but what I've got I'll give to you. } 'Cause

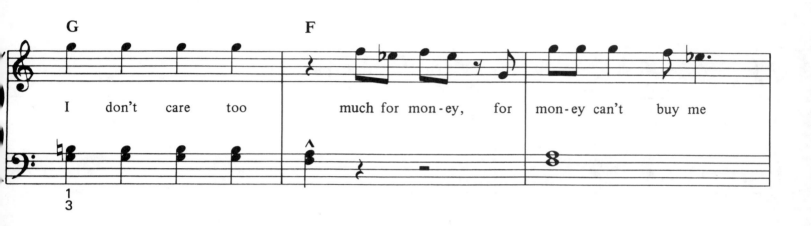

I don't care too much for mon-ey, for mon-ey can't buy me

love. I'll love. Can't buy me love, _____

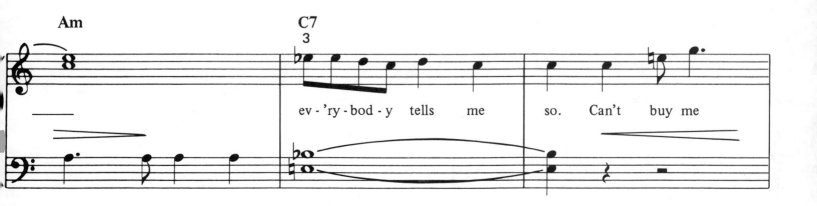

__ ev-'ry-bod-y tells me so. Can't buy me

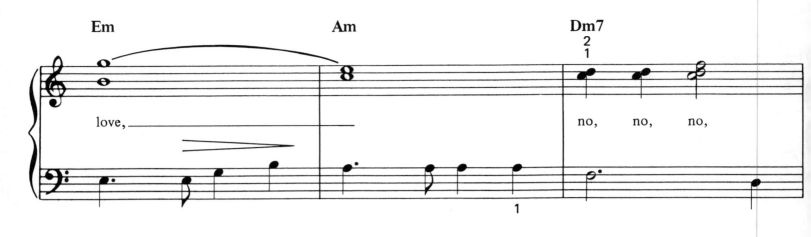

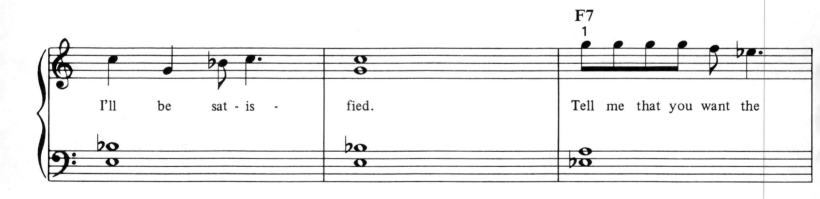

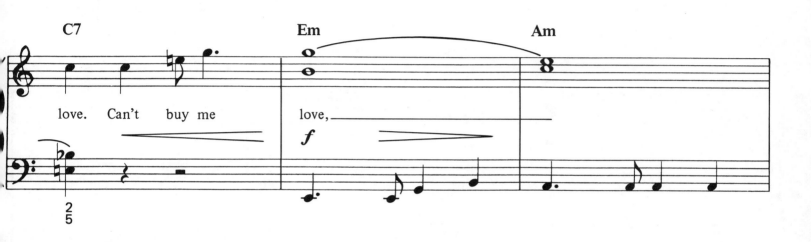

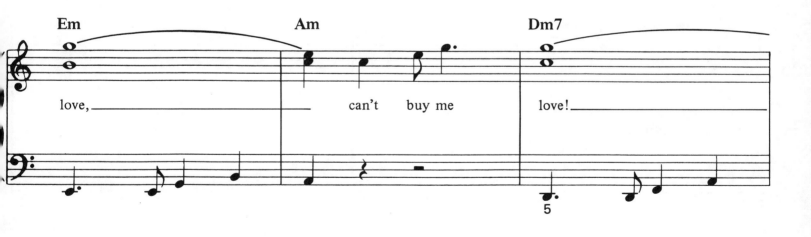

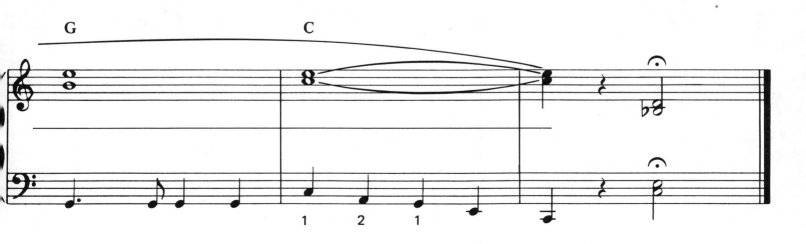

CHAINS

Words and Music by GERRY GOFFIN
and CAROLE KING

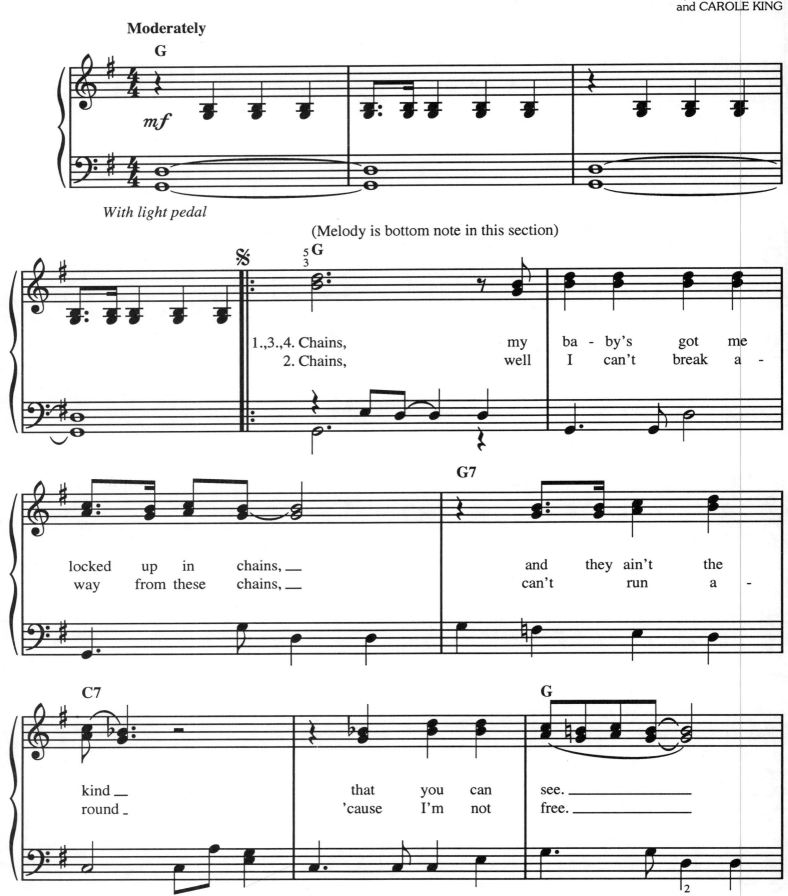

DON'T BE CRUEL
(To A Heart That's True)

Words and Music by OTIS BLACKWELL
and ELVIS PRESLEY

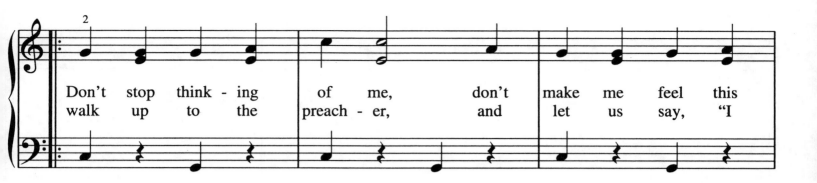

Don't stop think - ing of me, don't make me feel this
walk up to the preach - er, and let us say, "I

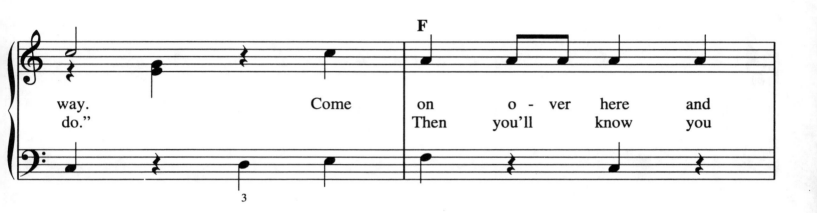

F

way. Come on o - ver here and
do." Then you'll know and you

C

love me. You know what I want you to
have me, and I'll know I'll have you,

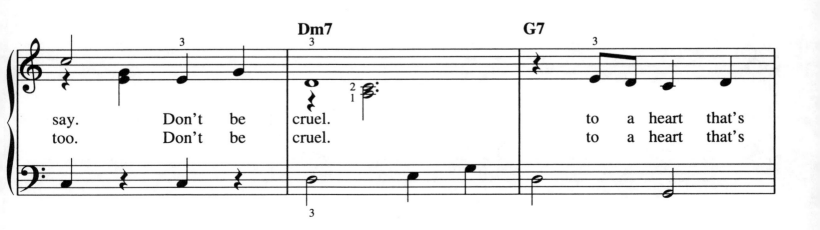

Dm7   G7

say. Don't be cruel. to a heart that's
too. Don't be cruel. to a heart that's

45

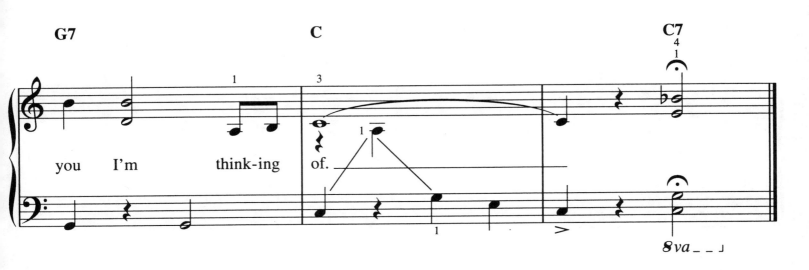

DREAM LOVER

Words and Music by
BOBBY DARIN

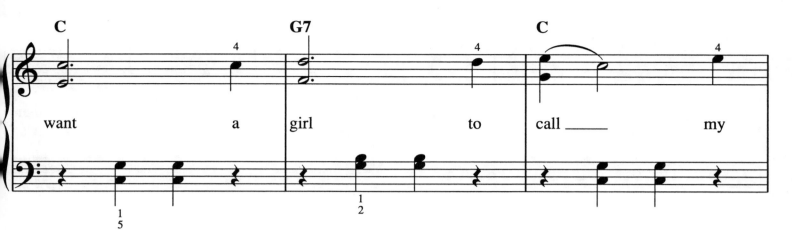

want   a   girl   to   call _____   my

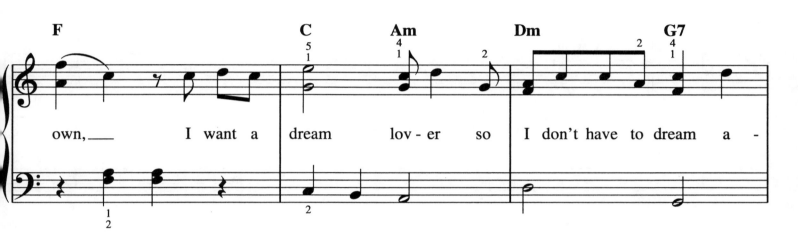

own, ___   I want a   dream   lov - er   so   I don't have to dream   a -

lone.   Dream lov - er,
                                                     Dream lov - er,

where are   you _____   with a love,   oh, so   true, __
un - til   then _____   I'll go to sleep and   dream a - gain. __

lone.

Some day,   I

don't know how, _____   I hope you'll   hear my   plea.__

Some way,   I   don't know how, ____   she'll bring her

love to me. _

D.S. al Coda

CODA

lone.

GOODBYE CRUEL WORLD

Words and Music by
GLORIA SHAYNE

51

53

Let the peo-ple point at me and stare. I'll tell the world that wom-an, wher-

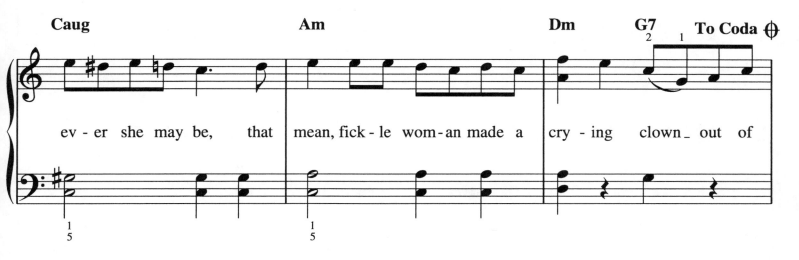

ev - er she may be, that mean, fick - le wom-an made a cry - ing clown_ out of

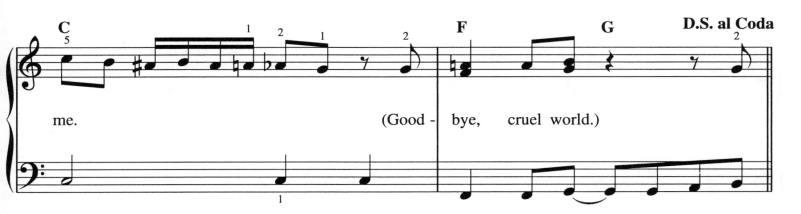

me. (Good - bye, cruel world.)

me. Good - bye cruel world.

GREAT BALLS OF FIRE

Words and Music by OTIS BLACKWELL
and JACK HAMMER

A GROOVY KIND OF LOVE

Words and Music by TONI WINE
and CAROLE BAYER SAGER

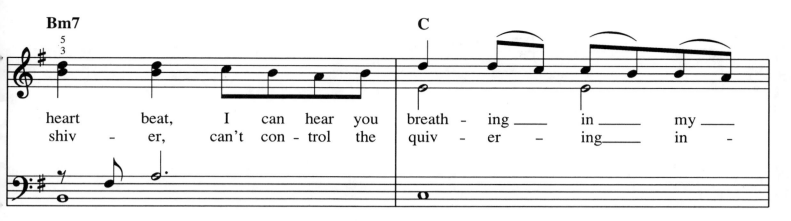

Bm7 ... C

heart beat, I can hear you | breath - ing ____ in ____ my ____
shiv - er, can't con - trol the | quiv - er - ing ____ in -

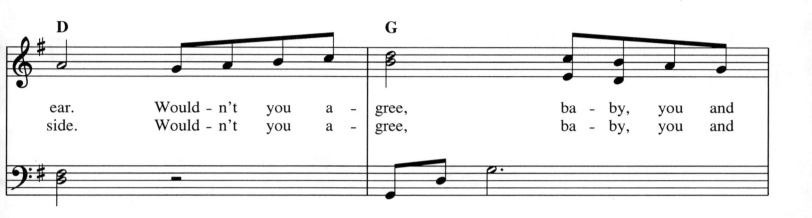

D ... G

ear. Would - n't you a - gree, | ba - by, you and
side. Would - n't you a - gree, | ba - by, you and

D/G ... 1. G ... D

me got a groo-vy kind of | love. | An - y-time you
me got a groo-vy kind of

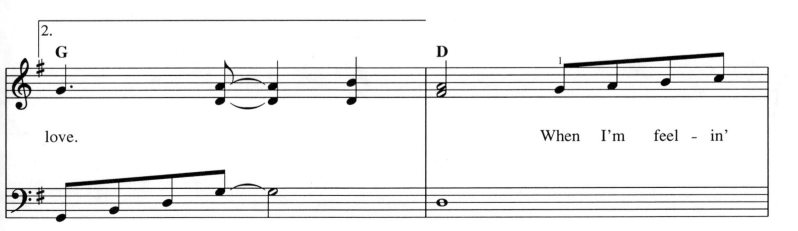

2. G ... D

love. | When I'm feel - in'

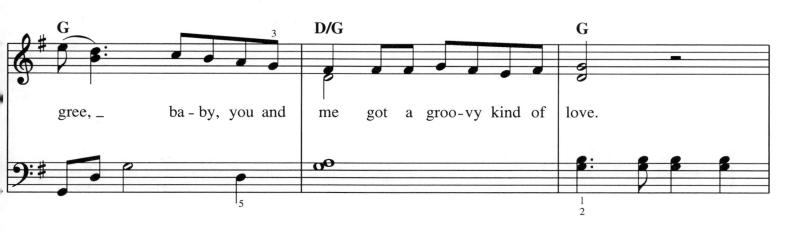

gree, _ ba - by, you and me got a groo-vy kind of love.

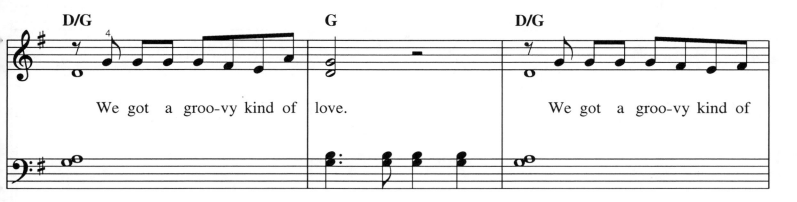

We got a groo-vy kind of love. We got a groo-vy kind of

love.

We got a groo-vy kind of love.

rit.

HIPPY HIPPY SHAKE

Words and Music by
CHAN ROMERO

I GOT YOU
(I Feel Good)

Words and Music by
JAMES BROWN

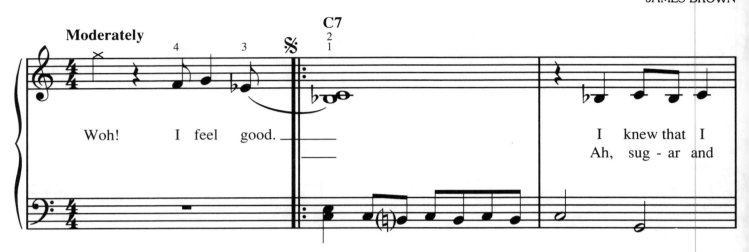

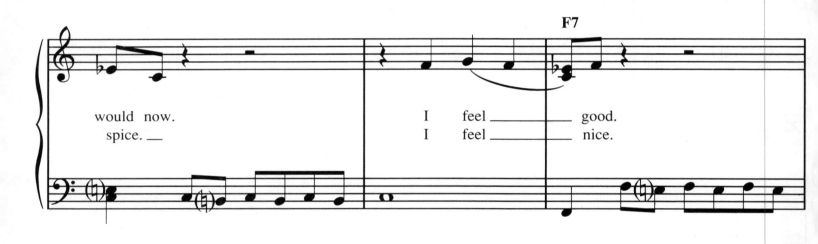

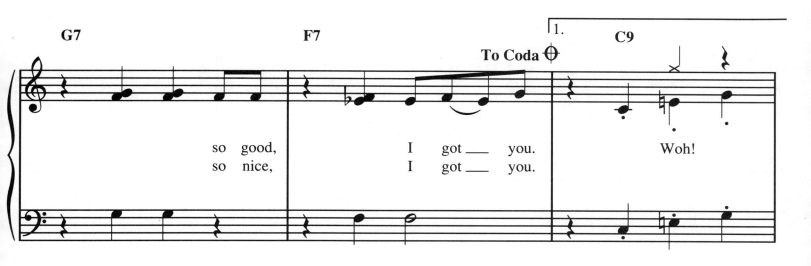

so good,
so nice,
I got ___ you.
I got ___ you.
Woh!

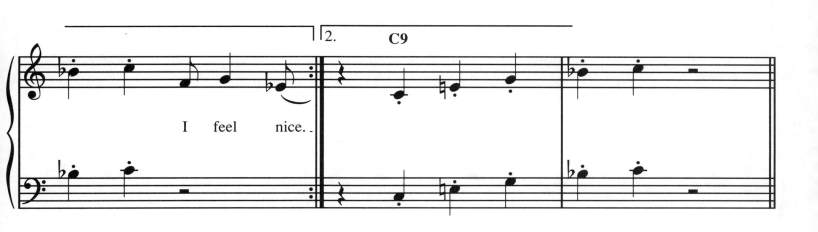

I feel nice.

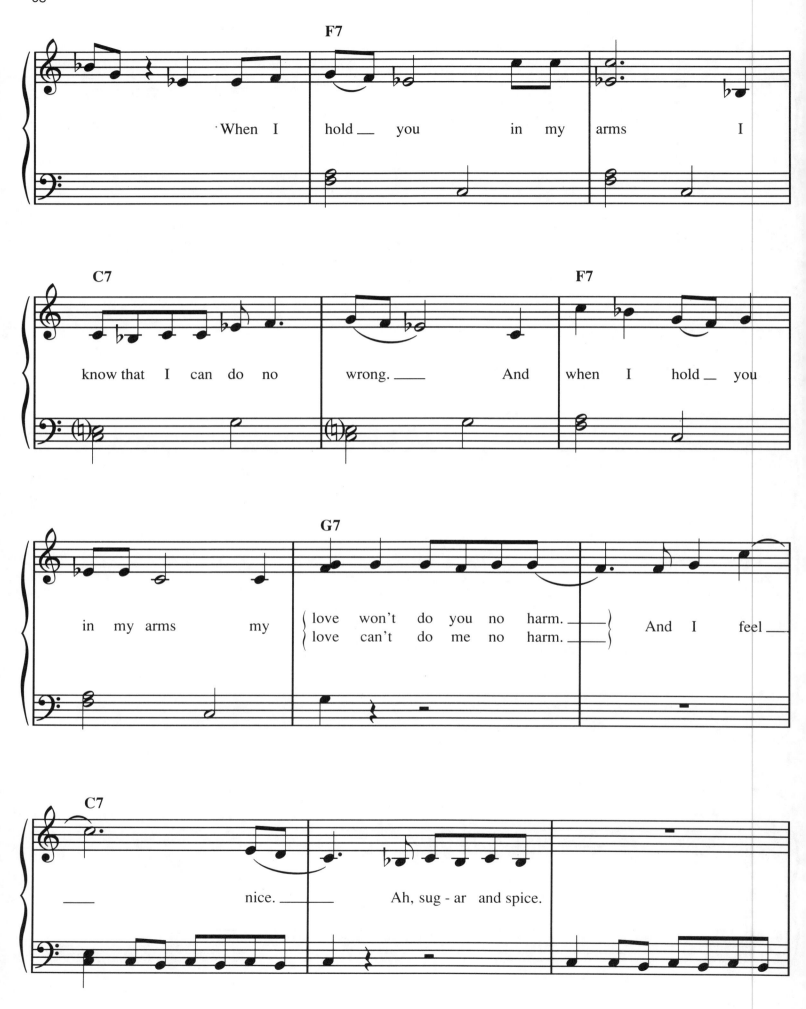

IT HURTS TO BE IN LOVE

Words and Music by HELEN MILLER
and HOWARD GREENFIELD

72

IT'S MY PARTY

Words and Music by HERB WIENER,
WALLY GOLD and JOHN GLUCK, JR.

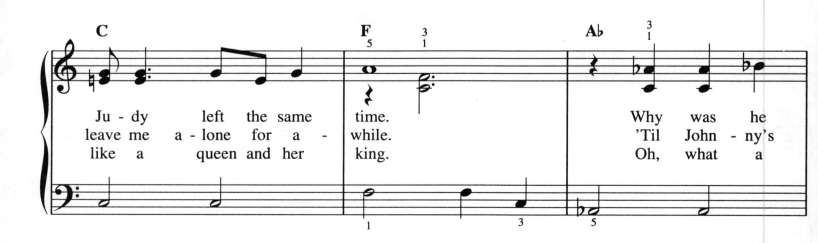

8va

THE LOCO-MOTION

Words and Music by GERRY GOFFIN
and CAROLE KING

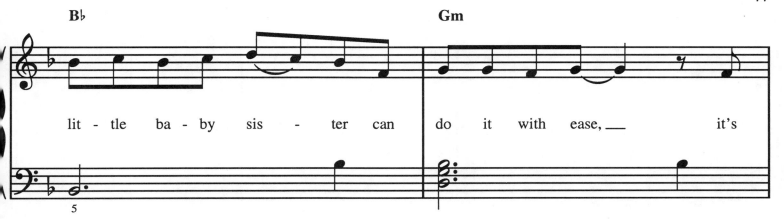

lit - tle ba - by sis - ter can do it with ease, ___ it's

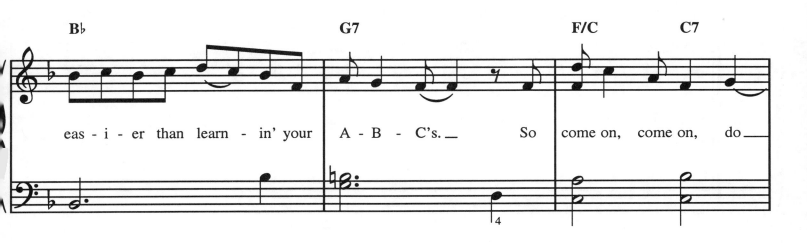

eas - i - er than learn - in' your A - B - C's. ___ So come on, come on, do ___

___ the lo - co - mo - tion with me. You got - ta swing your hips now.

Come on ba - by jump up, ___ jump back. ___

78

LOVE ME DO

Moderate Rock

Words and Music by JOHN LENNON
and PAUL McCARTNEY

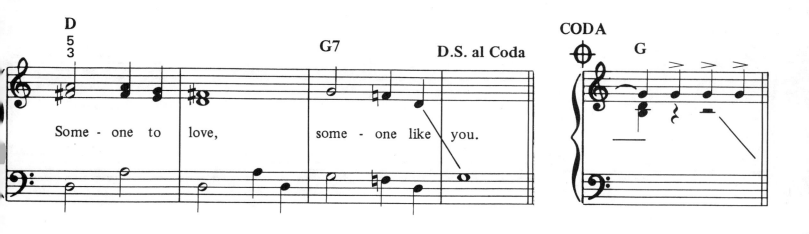

LEADER OF THE PACK

Words and Music by GEORGE MORTON,
JEFF BARRY and ELLIE GREENWICH

Ad lib.

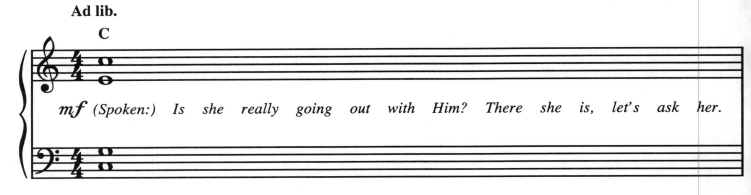

mf (Spoken:) Is she really going out with Him? There she is, let's ask her.

With pedal

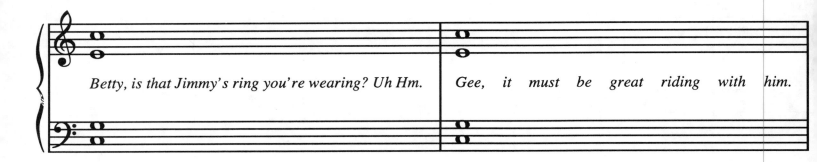

Betty, is that Jimmy's ring you're wearing? Uh Hm.   Gee, it must be great riding with him.

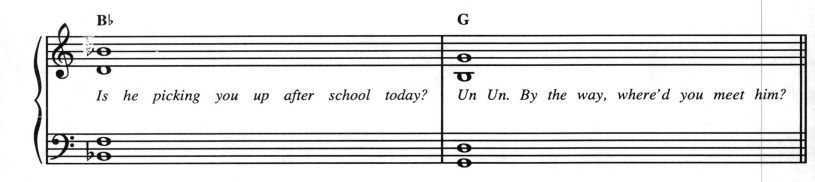

Is he picking you up after school today?   Un Un. By the way, where'd you meet him?

Moderately with a beat

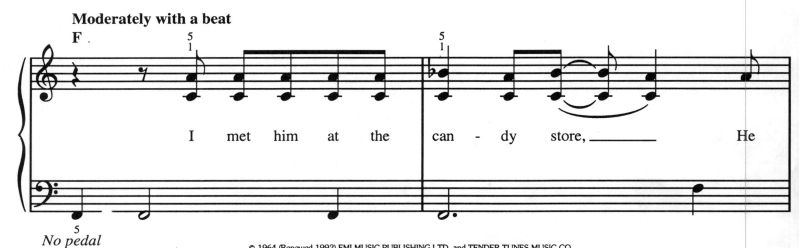

I met him at the   can - dy store, _____   He

No pedal

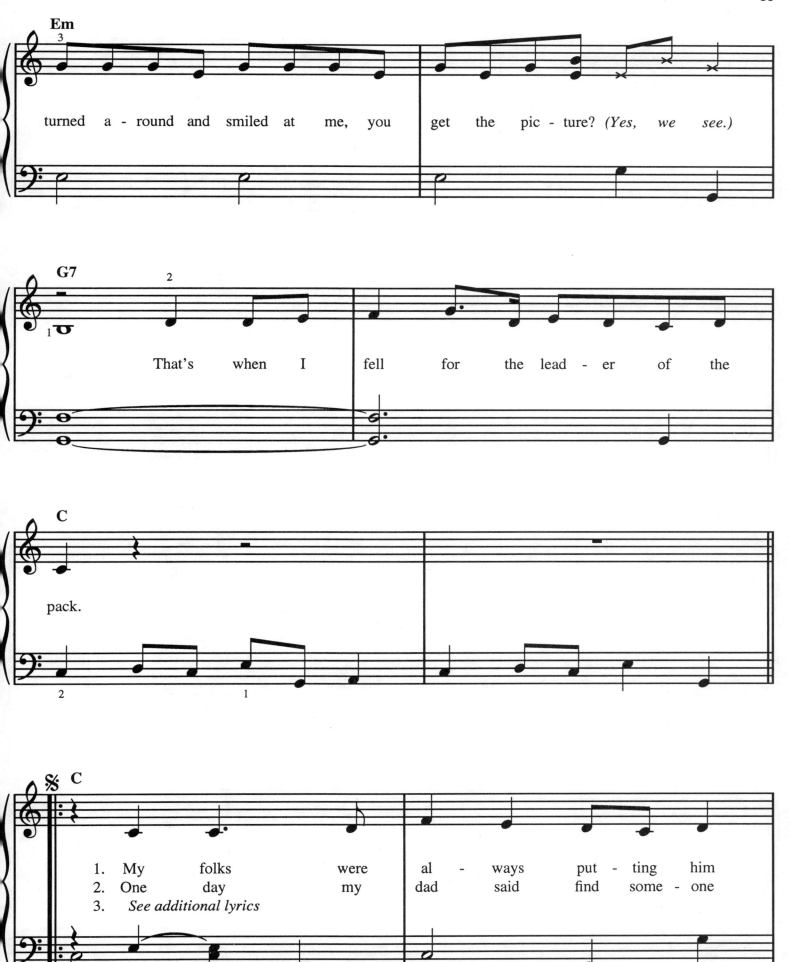

Em

turned a - round and smiled at me, you get the pic - ture? *(Yes, we see.)*

G7

That's when I fell for the lead - er of the

C

pack.

% **C**

1. My folks were al - ways put - ting him
2. One day my dad said find some - one
3. *See additional lyrics*

(No pedal)

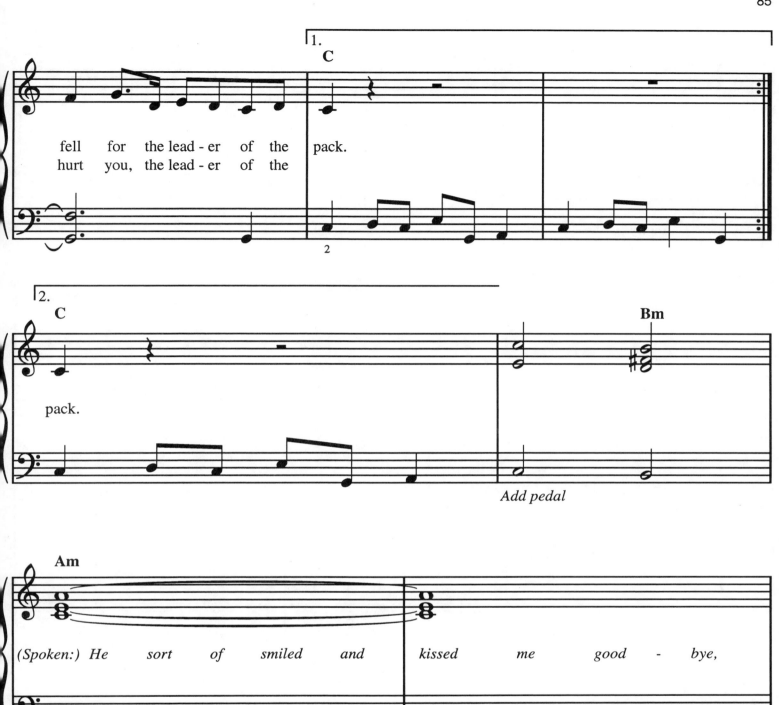

1.

C

fell for the lead - er of the pack.
hurt you, the lead - er of the

2.

C

pack.

Bm

Add pedal

Am

(Spoken:) He sort of smiled and kissed me good - bye,

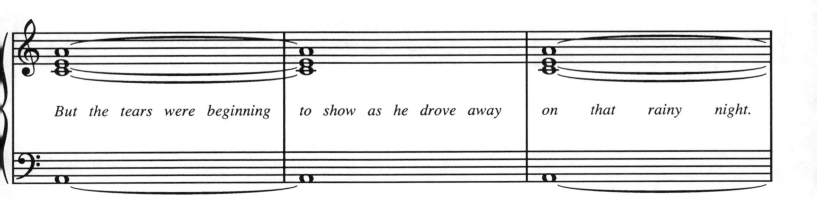

But the tears were beginning to show as he drove away on that rainy night.

Additional Lyrics

3. I felt so helpless, what could I do?
Rememb'ring all the things we'd been through.

MAGGIE MAY

Words and Music by ROD STEWART
and MARTIN QUITTENTON

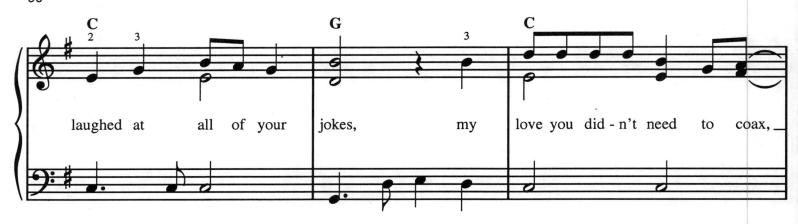

laughed at all of your jokes, my love you did-n't need to coax,

Oh, Mag-gie, I could-n't have tried _____ an - y

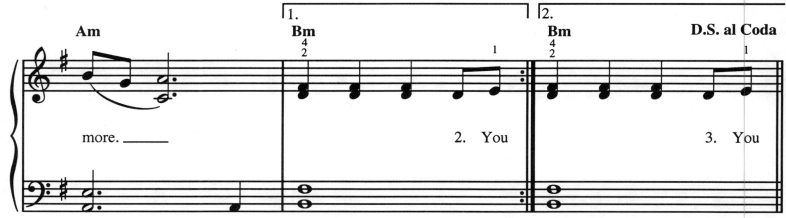

more. _____ 2. You 3. You

face. _____ You made a first - class fool out of

me, but I'm as blind as a fool can be, _____ you

stole my heart _ but I love you an - y - way. _____

Repeat and Fade

(Shouted:) Maggie, I wish I'd never seen your face. I'll
get on back home one of those days.

Additional Lyrics

2. You lured me away from home, just to save you from being alone.
   You stole my soul, that's a pain I can do without.
   All I needed was a friend to lend a guiding hand.
   But you turned into a lover, and, Mother, what a lover! You wore me out.
   All you did was wreck my bed, and in the morning kick me in the head.
   Oh, Maggie, I couldn't have tried any more.

3. You lured me away from home, 'cause you didn't want to be alone.
   You stole my heart, I couldn't leave you if I tried.
   I suppose I could collect my books and get back to school.
   Or steal my Daddy's cue and make a living out of playing pool,
   Or find myself a rock and roll band that needs a helpin' hand.
   Oh, Maggie, I wish I'd never seen your face. **(To Coda)**

MAGIC CARPET RIDE

Words and Music by JOHN KAY
and RUSHTON MOREVE

(You've Got)
THE MAGIC TOUCH

Words and Music by
BUCK RAM

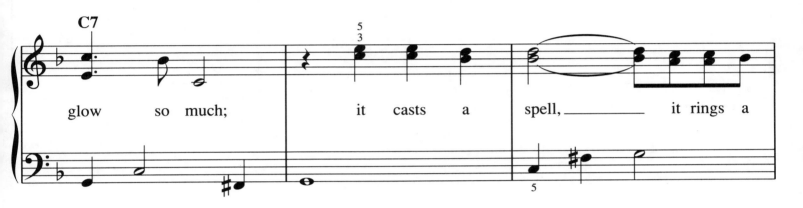

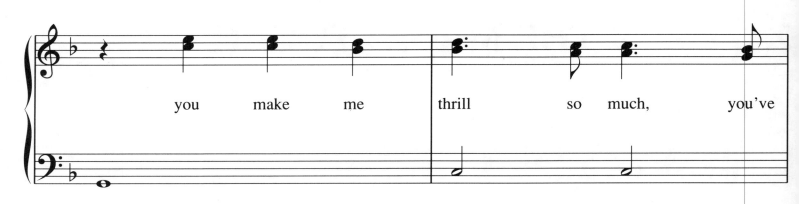

you make me thrill so much, you've

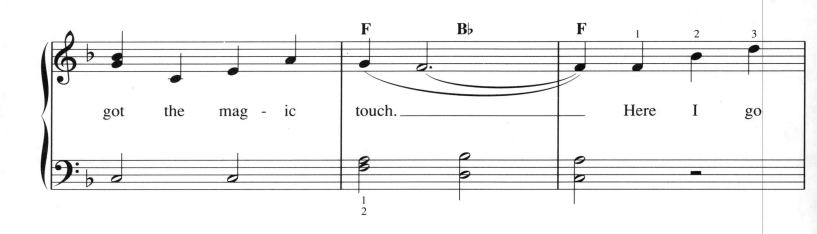

got the mag - ic touch. _____ Here I go

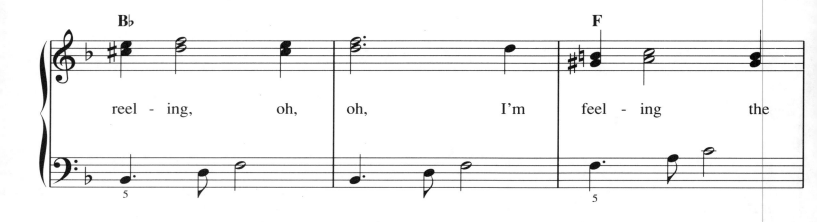

reel - ing, oh, oh, I'm feel - ing the

glow, but where can I go from

you?_____ I did-n't know too much, _____

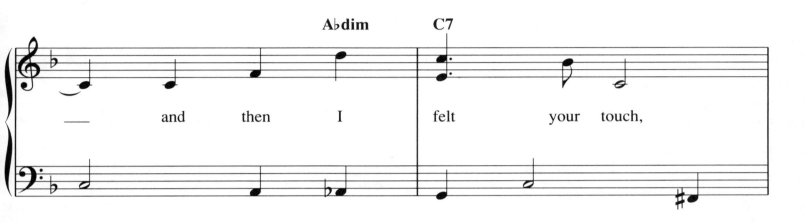

___ and then I felt your touch,

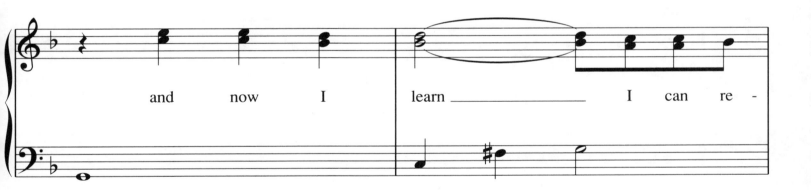

and now I learn_____ I can re-

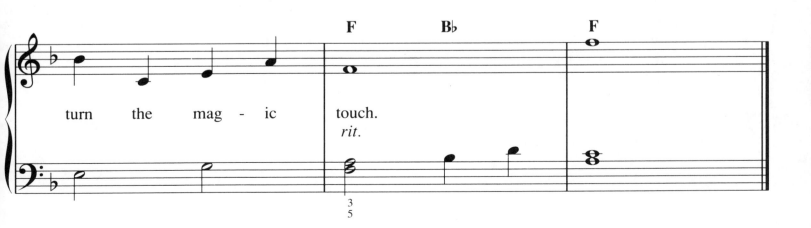

turn the mag - ic touch.
rit.

MAMA TOLD ME
(Not To Come)

Words and Music by
RANDY NEWMAN

With a heavy beat

MY BOYFRIEND'S BACK

Words and Music by ROBERT FELDMAN,
GERALD GOLDSTEIN and RICHARD GOTTEHRER

OH! CAROL

Words and Music by HOWARD GREENFIELD
and NEIL SEDAKA

ON BROADWAY

Words and Music by BARRY MANN, CYNTHIA WEIL,
MIKE STOLLER and JERRY LEIBER

They say the ne - on lights are bright on
They say the wo - men treat you fine on
They say that I won't last too long on

Broad - way; they say there's al - ways
Broad - way, but look - in' at them
Broad - way. I'll catch a Grey-hound

mag - ic in the air.
just gives me the blues.
bus for home they say.

ONE FINE DAY

Words and Music by GERRY GOFFIN
and CAROLE KING

meant to
walking by
be. _____
your side. _____

One fine

day _____

you're gon-na

want me for your

1.

girl.

girl.

some _____ day dar - ling, ___ you'll come to

$\frac{1}{2}$

D.S. al Coda

me when you ___ want to set - tle down, oh.

CODA

girl. One fine day, _____

1

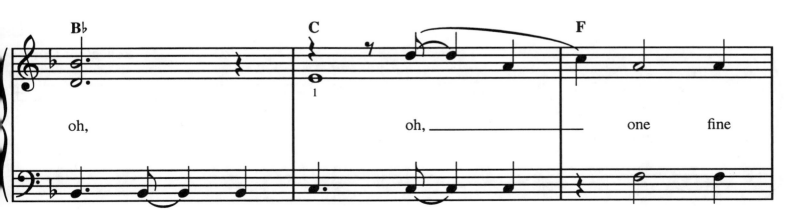

oh, oh, _____ one fine

day _____ you're gon - na want me for your

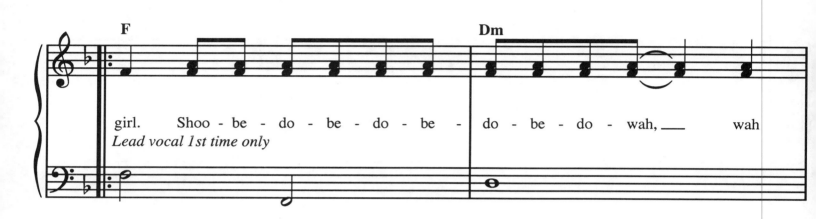

girl. Shoo - be - do - be - do - be - do - be - do - wah, ___ wah
Lead vocal 1st time only

shoo - be - do - be - do - be - do - be - do - wah, ___ wah.

Instrumental ad lib. and fade

Repeat and Fade

PEOPLE GOT TO BE FREE

Words and Music by FELIX CAVALIERE
and EDWARD BRIGATI, JR.

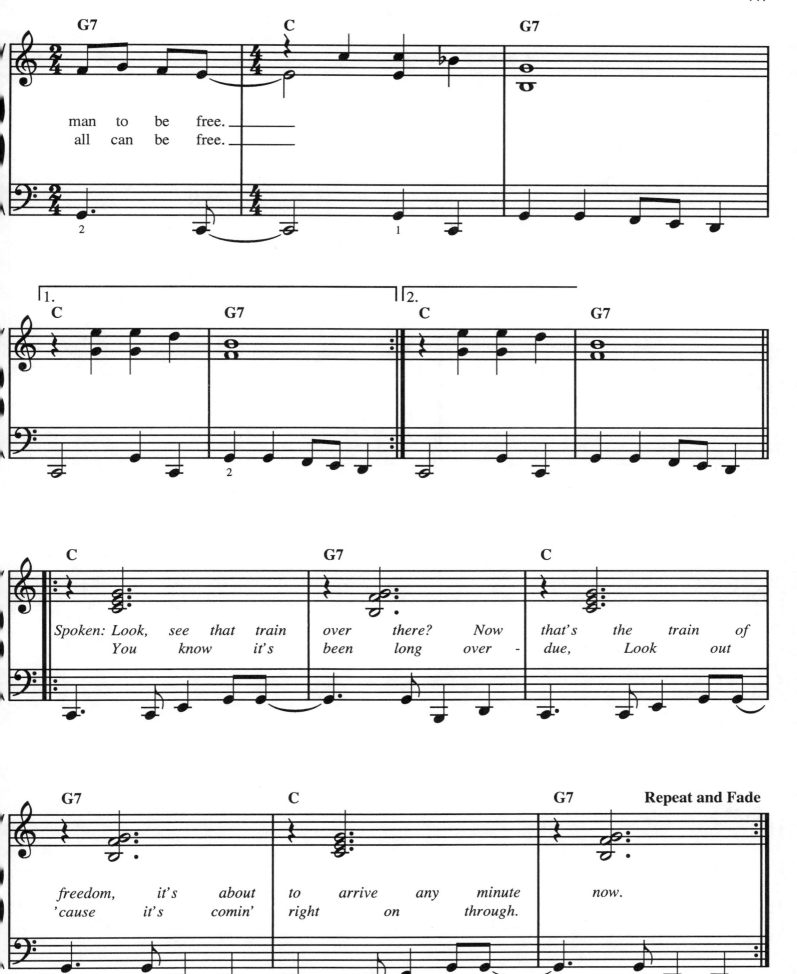

PRECIOUS AND FEW

Words and Music by
WALTER D. NIMS

share.   Pre-cious and few __ are the

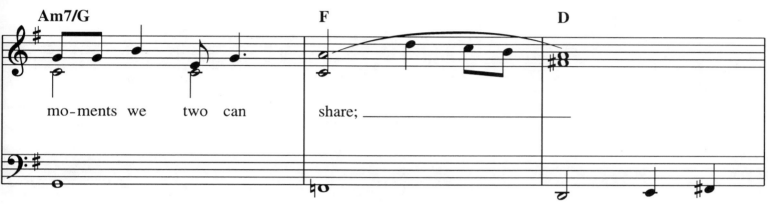

mo-ments we   two can   share; _____

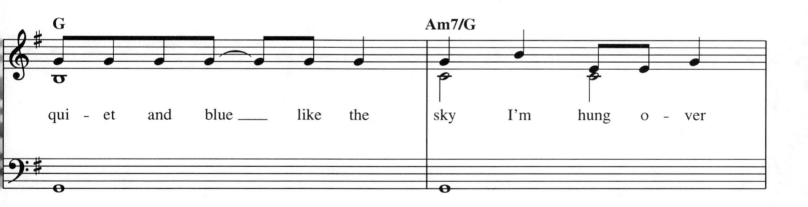

qui - et and blue __ like the   sky   I'm   hung o - ver

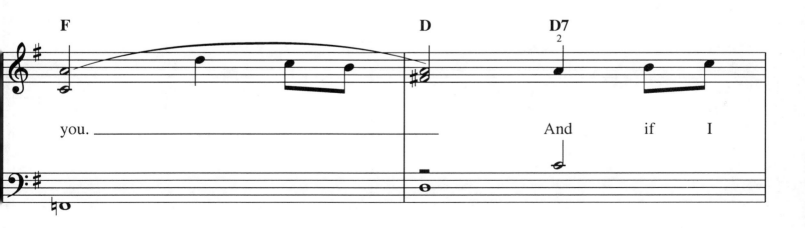

you. _____   And   if   I

PRETTY LITTLE ANGEL EYES

Words and Music by TOMMY BOYCE
and CURTIS LEE

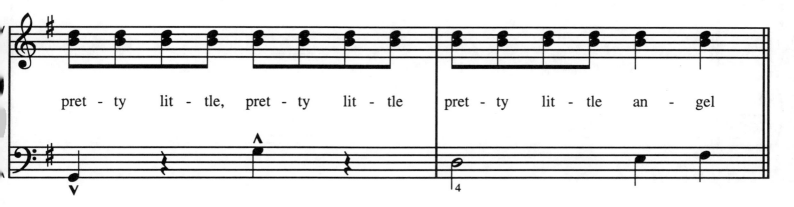

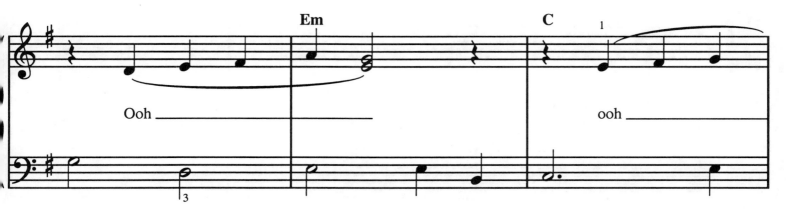

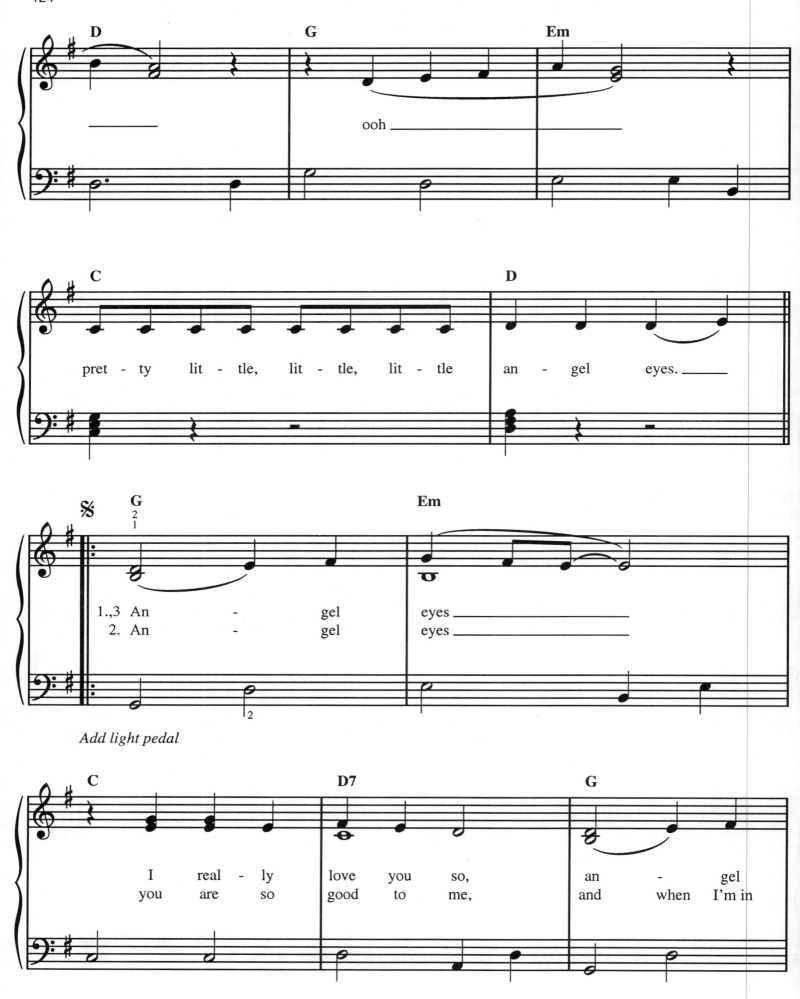

ooh

pret - ty lit - tle, lit - tle, lit - tle an - gel eyes.

1.,3 An - gel eyes
2. An - gel eyes

Add light pedal

I real - ly love you so, an - gel
you are so good to me, and when I'm in

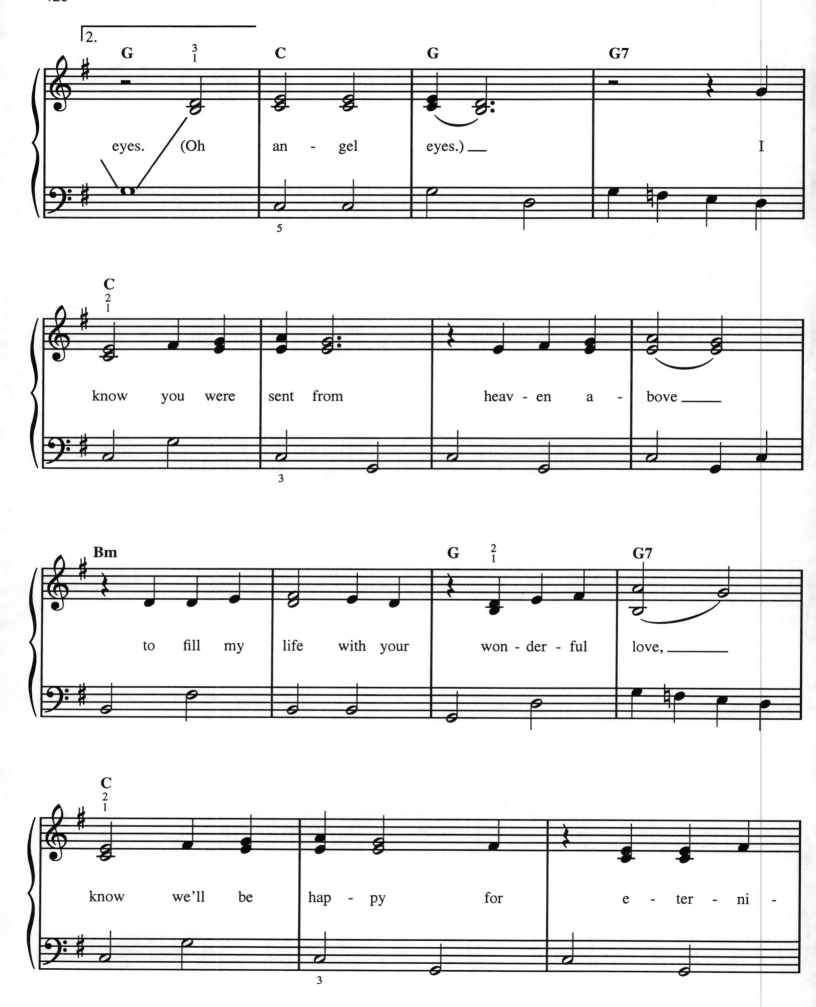

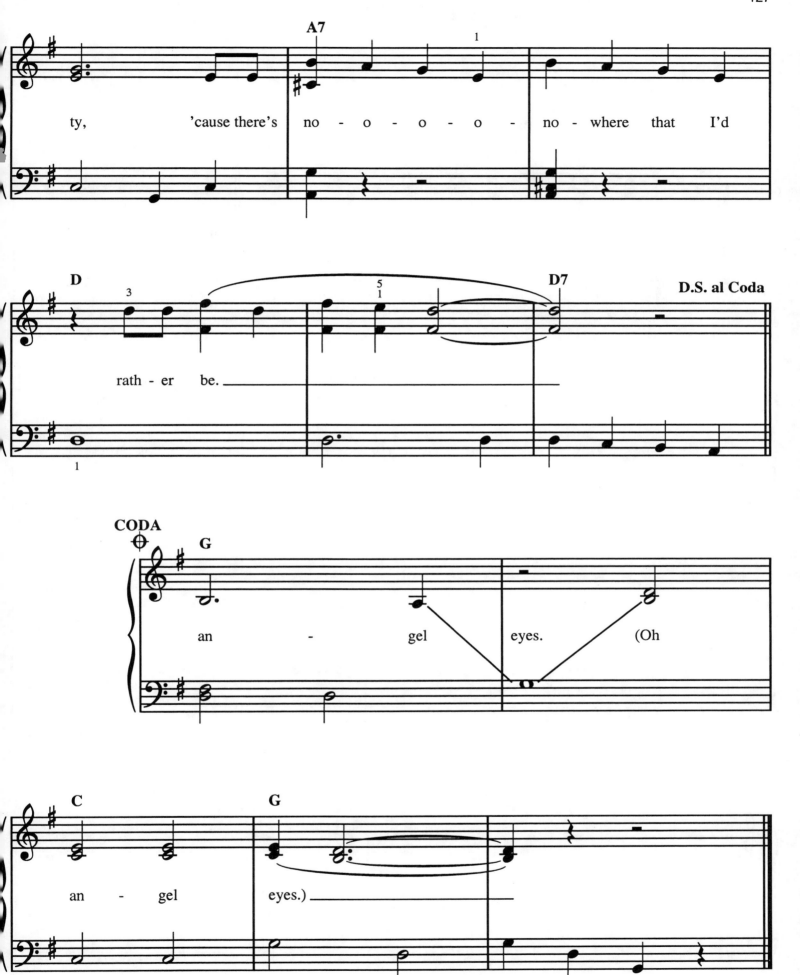

ROCK AROUND THE CLOCK

By MAX C. FREEDMAN
and JIMMY DeKNIGHT

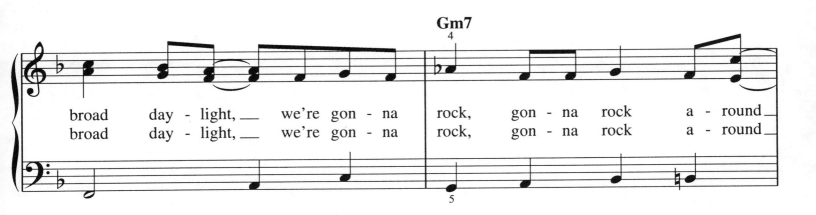

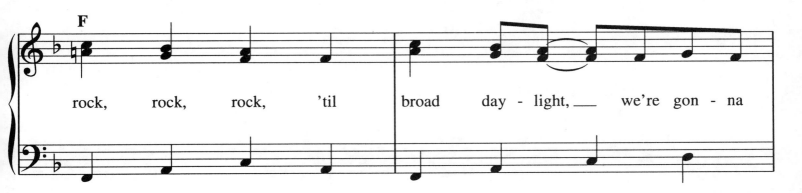

Additional Lyrics

3. When the clock strikes twelve, we'll cool off, then,
   Start a rockin' 'round the clock again,
   We're gonna rock around the clock tonight,
   We're gonna rock, rock, rock, 'til broad daylight,
   We're gonna rock, gonna rock around the clock tonight.

THE SHOOP SHOOP SONG
(It's In His Kiss)

Words and Music by
RUDY CLARK

133

SPLISH SPLASH

Words and Music by BOBBY DARIN
and JEAN MURRAY

STUPID CUPID

Words and Music by HOWARD GREENFIELD
and NEIL SEDAKA

139

SURF CITY

Words and Music by BRIAN WILSON
and JAN BERRY

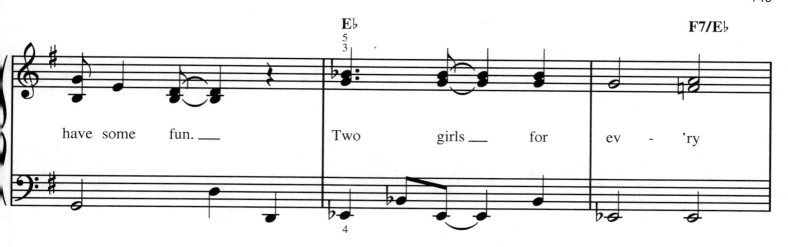

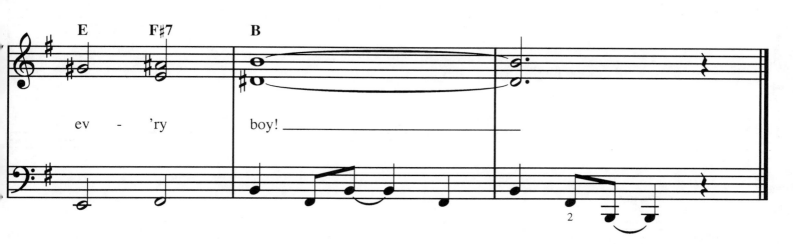

Additional Lyrics

3. And if my woody breaks down on me somewhere on my surf route,
   Surf City here we come!
   I'll strap my board to my back and hitch a ride in my wet suit.
   Surf City here we come!
   When I get to Surf City I'll be shootin' the curl
   and pickin' out the parties for the surfer girl.

SWEET TALKIN' GUY

Words and Music by DOUG MORRIS, ELLIOT GREENBERG,
BARBARA BAER and ROBERT SCHWARTZ

TICKET TO RIDE

Words and Music by JOHN LENNON
and PAUL McCARTNEY

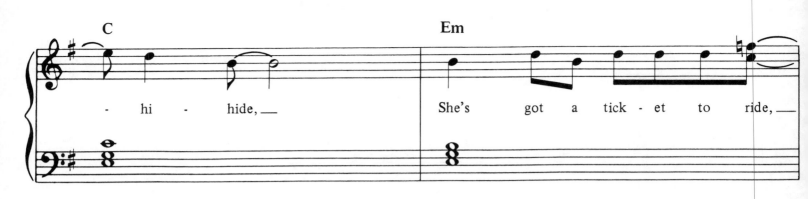

- hi - hide, ___ She's got a tick - et to ride, ___

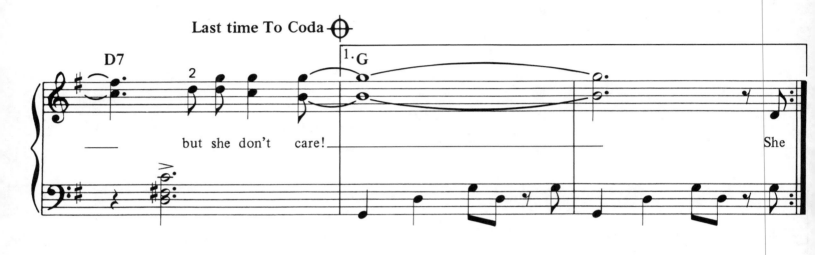

Last time To Coda

___ but she don't care! ___ She

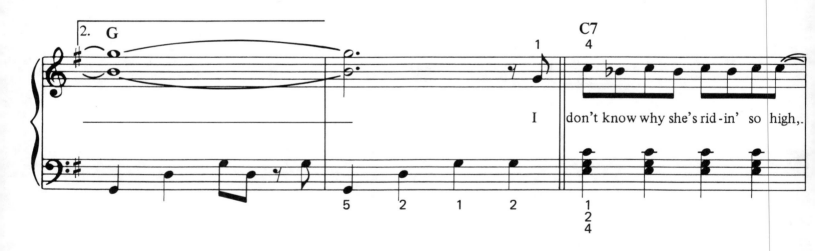

I don't know why she's rid-in' so high, ___

___ she ought-ta think twice she ought-ta do right by

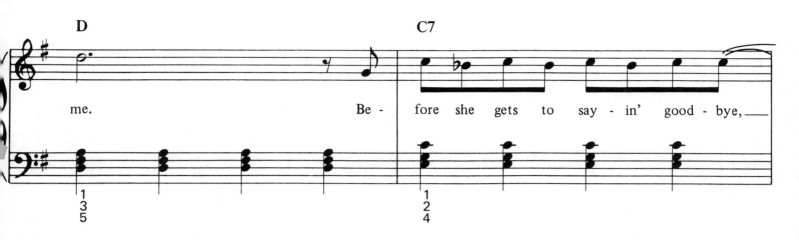

me.   Be - fore she gets to say - in' good - bye,____

____ she ought-ta think twice,   she ought-ta do right   by

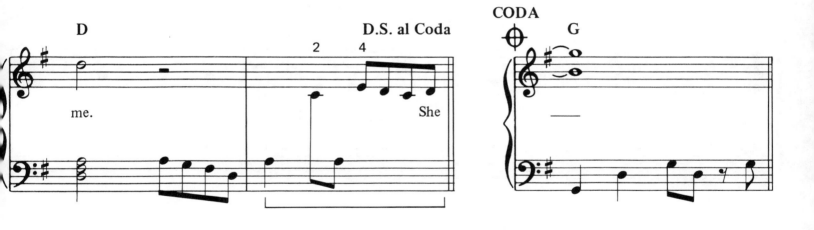

me.   She

CODA

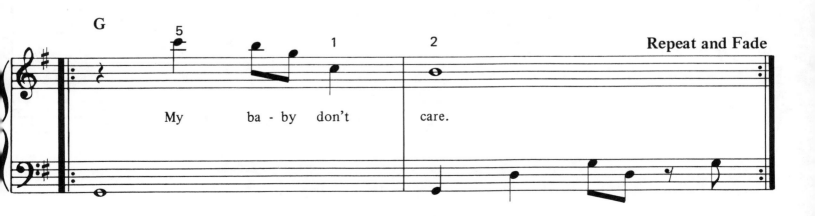

My   ba - by   don't   care.

Repeat and Fade

TEQUILA

By CHUCK RIO

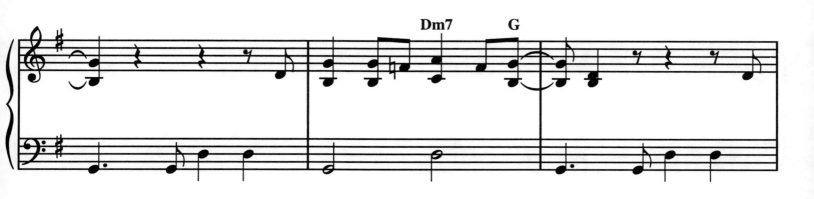

Spoken: Tequila!

153

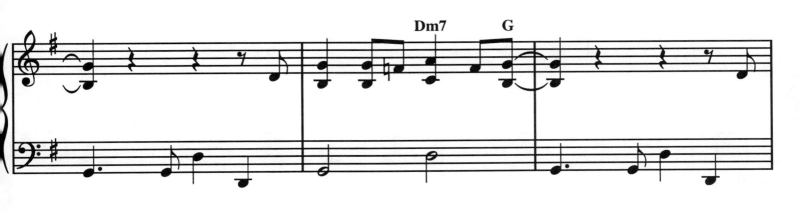

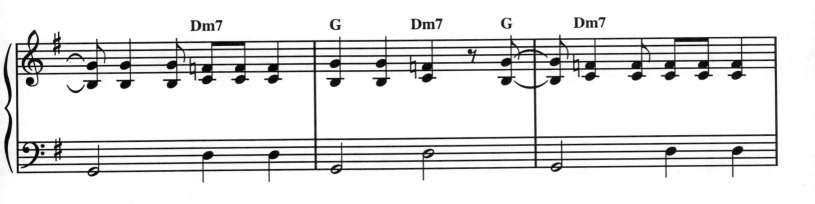

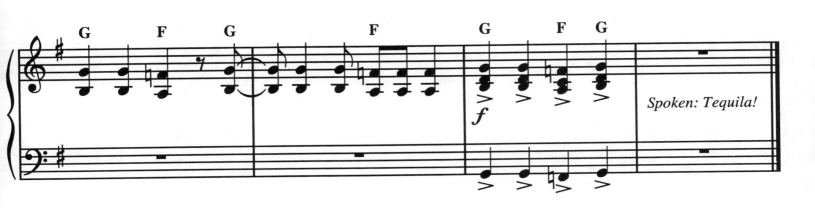

Spoken: Tequila!

TWIST AND SHOUT

Words and Music by BERT RUSSELL
and PHIL MEDLEY

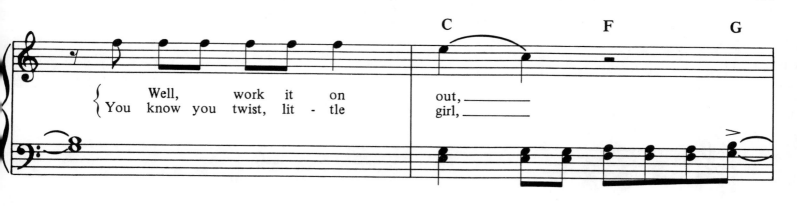

Well, work it on out, ___
You know you twist, lit - tle girl, ___

You know you look so good; ___ You know you got ___ me ___
You know you twist so fine ___ Come on and twist a lit - tle

go - in' now, Just like I knew you would.
clos - er now, And let me know that you're mine.

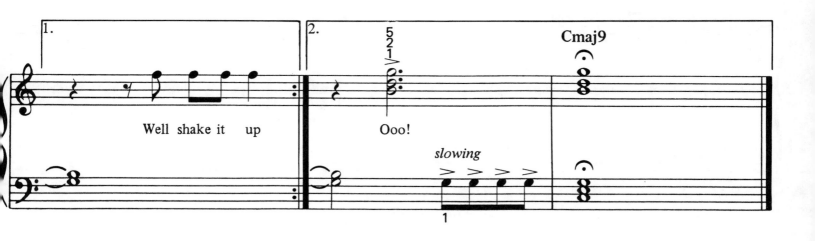

1.
Well shake it up

2.
Ooo!

slowing

Cmaj9

UP ON THE ROOF

Words and Music by GERRY GOFFIN
and CAROLE KING

At night the stars ___ put on a show for free, _____ and dar - ling, you ___ can share it all ___ with me. _____

WILD THING

Words and Music by
CHIP TAYLOR

WOMAN, WOMAN

Words and Music by JIM GLASER
and JIMMY PAYNE

1. Some - thing's wrong be - tween us _____ that your
2. I've seen the way men look at you when
3. (See additional lyrics)

laugh - ter can - not hide see And
they think I don't And it

you're a - fraid to let your ___ eyes meet
hurts to have to them think that ___ you're that

165

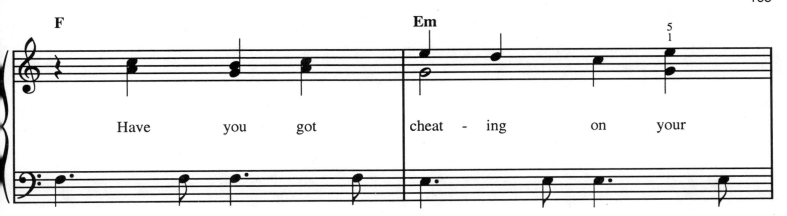

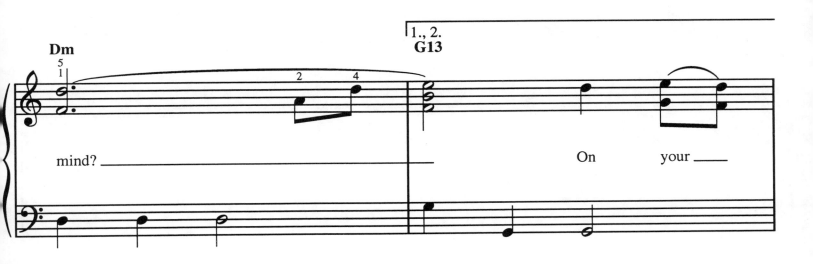

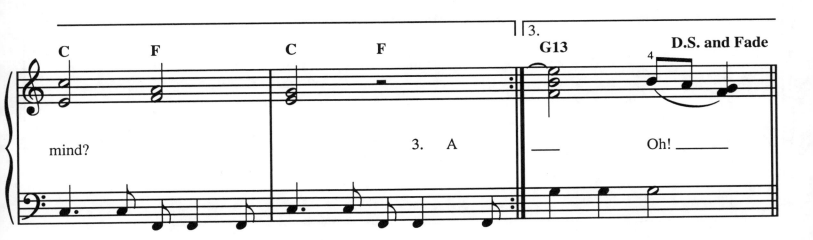

Additional Lyrics

3. A woman wears a certain look when she is on the move
And the man can always tell what's on her mind.
I hate to have to say it, but their looks are over you.
CHORUS

WILL YOU LOVE ME TOMORROW

(a/k/a Will You Still Love Me Tomorrow)

Words and Music by GERRY GOFFIN
and CAROLE KING

168

Additional Lyrics

3. I'd like to know that your love is love I can be sure of.
   So tell me now and I won't ask again.

WOOLY BULLY

Words and Music by
DOMINGO SAMUDIO

With a steady rock beat

Additional Lyrics

2. Hatty told Matty
   Let's don't take no chance.
   Let's not be L 7,
   Come and learn to dance.
   Wooly Bully, Wooly Bully.
   Wooly Bully, Wooly Bully, Wooly Bully.

3. Matty told Hatty
   That's the thing to do.
   Get yo' someone really
   To pull the wool with you.
   Wooly Bully, Wooly Bully.
   Wooly Bully, Wooly Bully, Wooly Bully.

YOU'VE LOST THAT LOVIN' FEELIN'

Words and Music by BARRY MANN,
CYNTHIA WEIL and PHIL SPECTOR